PRAISE FOR
When My Heart Goes Dark, I Turn the Porch Light On
by Jane Underwood

"With grace and humor, Jane Underwood presents in this collection the routine and terrifying advance of cancer. Does anyone want to read about this? In poetry? Yes—because why turn away from articulate courage and soulful craft. The days and years collected here also include all the other aspects of life: a dog pounding her tail, a hand-painted platter, jasmine blooms, love. Take heart in this posthumous collection so as to turn your own porch light on."

　　—Kimiko Hahn, Author of *Brain Fever*

"Lots of people get cancer and die. Not many write poems under those circumstances. Jane Underwood did. They're full of life. And also Portuguese macaroni."

　　—Will Walker, Author of *Wednesday After Lunch*

"Sharp, poignant, funny, tough, tart, sweet—like Jane herself, who lived life on her own terms and sang about it."

　　—Alison Luterman, Author of *Desire Zoo*

Jane Underwood's poems gaze at a fragile world of kith and kin, delivery guys, infusion nurses, leaves plastered to a sidewalk, inscrutable dead parents, and even victims of terrorism, an ocean away. Forged in the aftermath of a metastatic cancer diagnosis, these intimate poems can't help themselves: they keep stumbling into wonder, humor, absurdity, and tenderness, even in the most unpromising circumstances. Underwood knew just how quickly a life can become provisional, but while her poems look squarely at the body's hard truths, they never stop cherishing the cracked world. The vision here is so precise, the ear so acute, with a sense of juxtaposition so nimble, that even at their darkest, these poems radiate beauty.

WHEN MY HEART GOES DARK, I TURN THE PORCH LIGHT ON

Jane Underwood

BLUE LIGHT PRESS ❖ 1ST WORLD PUBLISHING

1ST WORLD
PUBLISHING

SAN FRANCISCO ❖ FAIRFIELD ❖ DELHI

When My Heart Goes Dark, I Turn the Porch Light On
Copyright ©2017 by **Jane Underwood**

1st World Library
PO Box 2211
Fairfield, IA 52556
www.1stworldpublishing.com

Blue Light Press
www.bluelightpress.com
Email: bluelightpress@aol.com

Book & Cover Design
Melanie Gendron
www.melaniegendron.com

Cover Art
Jane Underwood

Author Photograph
Beverly Tharp

First Edition

ISBN 978-1-4218-3780-2

FOR WILL
&
FOR JACK

ACKNOWLEDGEMENTS

There was many a time during the course of putting this book together that I came to tears, or nearly did. It wasn't just because I missed my Janie or because I knew she would love that this book of her poems has come to reality. At times, my emotions got the best of me because of the people who helped to make it possible. So on behalf of myself, Jane's son Will and my Janie it is with the utmost love that I extend my appreciation.

To the people who supported Jane while she wrote these poems and saw to getting this project done — Karen Hildebrand, Julie Bruck and Kerry Campbell — thank you, thank you, thank you. I didn't have to put this team together; the rallying cry was "Oh yeah, these poems must get published! Let's do it!" Because of your love and respect for Jane and her work there was no stopping you.

Beverly Tharp, the photograph you took of Jane in the bay window is the best. I will always have it nearby. It captures Jane and her energy perfectly.

Kimiko Hahn, thank you for your blurb. It is deeply appreciated.

Alison Luterman and Will Walker, thank you, not just for your book cover comments, but also for your friendship.

All profits from the sale of *When My Heart Goes Dark, I Turn the Porch Light On* are to benefit breast cancer research.

—Jack Carroll

CONTENTS

I.

II.

III.

IV.

V.

VI.

VII.

• • •

I.

Everybody Has Their Plans

God has a rash.
A bad one. Spreading fast.
Hello monkey wrench.

Not the best time
for Him to have to deal
with those two new
comas—the girl on a bike,
hit by a car, the woman
in a lake, struck by a boat.
It's been six months
for the girl, plus eight
long surgeries.
The woman, well,
her children and their
father have just
released her ashes
into the harbor.

Goddamnit, says God.

Nobody gets
the ups and downs
of running a universe.

Now this.

Isn't being God Almighty
enough? *Jesus H. Christ.*

Everybody has their
plans for the weekend.
But not Him. Not a chance.
He's got this red, inflamed
and hellishly itching rash,
which is manifesting,
wouldn't you know it,
          as a beautiful dawn sky.

You Are Washing Something

A dirty tub. A dusty table.
The bug-spattered windshield.
A wine glass at your fifty-third
birthday party. You are
washing something. A floor.
Your face. A scar that is aching
and swollen and numb around
the edges. The cat licks her paw.
She is meticulous. Your high heel
is lying on its side, on the floor,
on top of the pathology report.
Your hair is cut shorter now than it
has ever been. You are washing
something. Tomorrow you will
wash your new short hair, which
will dry faster than before. Your
diagnosis is a maze of facts
impossible to decipher. You are
washing the mystery. Your pretty
shoe is lying on its side, on the
floor, on top of the word metastatic.
You are washing something.

The Talking Cancer Dress

The gauzy pink, cowl-necked dress
could expound for hours about
how difficult it was, what
a struggle it had been to exist,
hold on, to have made it this far . . .
but then again, what a gift!

How beautifully
it swirled around her body,
and spoke of what
it meant to bear the weight
of itself, about why it had
every right to kvetch, shed tears . . .
and yes, also every reason to rejoice!

Busy folks (loved ones, strangers, friends)
who were passing briefly by
stopped dead in their tracks whenever
the talking cancer dress held forth.
How tough it must be, they said,
then broke into applause, cheered,
tossed coins into her purse,
and just as quickly as they'd appeared,
dispersed.

Standing on the Corner

I wait
for my ride
to more needles,
x-rays, scans—
to that
        strip joint
where they
won't let
anyone hide.

Mutilated, bloated,
bruised.
Panting, bald,
exposed ... I wait
on a public street,
        dying
to run back home.

Suddenly
I am visited
by one
white
        butterfly.

It flits and floats
oblivious
to its audience,
a private dance

        a foot
        or so
        above the asphalt.

Just Call Me Cancer Woman

Cancer Woman never gets colds and can't make
heads or tails out of anything anymore.
Sneezer Woman (old friend) gets a cold every month
but never any awful diseases.
Cancer Woman can't do dinner with Sneezer Woman on Monday
because on Mondays all the restaurants are closed.
As if all the restaurants in the world must close their doors
in order to go fishing every Monday.
Sneezer Woman can't do dinner with Cancer Woman on Tuesday
because she'll be fasting after sunset.
As if all their dumb scheduling issues for the last thirty-five years
had been written into the stone pages of Foregone Conclusions.
Fucking Cat has taken to howling from the top
of Cancer Woman's laundry room cupboard.
Delivery Guy mixes up his 1's and r's, says *solly*,
de-rivered your box wrong house.

Cancer Woman assumes he escaped on a raft in the ocean.

No compass.

Fucking Cat refuses to come down on her own.

Know-It-All Doctor decrees:

Do what I say if you don't want to die.

As if Cancer Woman was a Fucking Cat stuck in a tree,

and he was the fire department.

Cancer Woman glares at Dr. Know-It-All.

As if he was a terrorist, a bank robber, or a god.

But he is just a guy who wears madras plaid.

Fucking Cat has gone berserk. As if she was totally lost

in her own house, stuck up there by the ceiling fan forever,

no firemen, no ladder, no gentle loving hands coming to save her.

Cancer Woman knows better. But she still feels wildly annoyed,

as if Fucking Cat, with her nine fucking lives,

has committed the ultimate crime by getting herself

into such a pickle.

All I Want

From behind a pane
of breath-fogged glass, I watch
          as you roll the trash bin
over the grass,
stop and start,
          start and stop.
You grip the rake, make piles
of what got said last night (words, mostly mine,
that swooped like hawks
then zeroed in).

          Towering above your head,
the biggest tree in our yard,
the one we thought at first was
just a bush that would be a breeze
to water and prune.

          But it grows and dies,
dies and grows in
          all directions, casting its shadow
over almost the entire yard.

          You're a man of few words (a trait
that often pains me) and you've gone outside
where there's no more need to talk or yell.

I'm the one who won the duel
and wears the crown.

I watch from on high
as you kneel in a patch of sun, pat the dirt,
smooth the ruffled lawn.

All I want
        is for you to look up
when I press my hand to the glass.

II.

To Do: Mastectomy

Come night you lay your head on pillows
Fat with severed wings. Come day you wake,
Dress, smooth the sheets, make the bed.

Cells once deemed your designated drivers
now stagger. Keys in hand, they weave
through blur. Who hid the goddamn car?

Everyone wants to know who you are—
last name first, date of birth, doctor,
diagnosis. *And is that right breast or left?*

In Keeping with the Rules of War

Breast *disappeared*
snatched off her chest
thrown
in an unmarked
bin.

Flesh *gone missing.*
Try to imagine
the surgeon's sword, the one
she saw in her head
before she went
under. Ten, nine, eight . . .
the glint.

Lesions on her spine
have begun to gnaw
at nearby nerves
that serve
as appetizers.

But so far
no bones
have been broken.

According to the doctors,
this means
       there has been no torture.

Song of Absence

First the scar
after the breast

then the presence
of the absence.

No words inscribed
upon a stone, no

place to lay down
flowers.

Poor, howling
chest.

How will she
reveal this

to the man
who has never been

without a merry tune
and cannot imagine

such a lonesome song.

Photo of a Garden
in a Mannequin

Did I over-crop her?
Doesn't she need a head?
Couldn't she have run away
if only she'd been spared
her legs? Nevermind.
Maybe they'll grow back.
But for now she's
the mannequin she
was meant to be, posed
behind a chipped but
golden wrought iron gate,
hand on hip, a saucy flirt.
A country garden has
taken root in her torso.
Photoshop, you rock.

She's got no organs,
true, but I'm her maker,
and this is my vision.
Butterflies and bees
have taken over.
Hummingbirds too.
It's a digital, impressionist
rendition of flowers in
a woman. It's a blur
of pastels with a blot of
red thrown in. It's how
I often see myself. It's
an exhibition, now open.

Saint Agatha of Sicily, 231-251 AD

As punishment for her defiance,
The Governor ordered them severed,
Then made her carry her breasts
On a platter, down the street.

Eventually her followers
Deemed their virgin martyress
The patron saint of bell makers.
Had her breasts been
Bell-like? Did a bell maker
See them on the platter
And feel inspired? Some say
She helped when Mount Etna
Erupted, was seen as a protector
Against the flames. Bells were
Fire alarms.

Later a band of bakers
Organized a feast, blessed
Bread loaves in her honor.
Had her breasts reminded them of
Hot cross buns? Communion wafers?

What platter would she have chosen,
I wonder, if given the option?
I'd have gone with my Southern
Blue Ridge from Appalachia,
Chipped and unsigned but
Painted by hand with flowers and
Lush ripe fruit—cherries, blueberries,
Apples, pears. One of a kind.

III.

Old Friend

Not a whine from
soft-spoken lesion, T-6
vertebrae, mid-spine.
Not a peep as I stand
and bend.

As for all you covert mets,
hiding in hips and other
secret spots, you are relentless,
yes, and yet you bide your
time. It's a strategic move,
I know, but I perceive it
as a form of tact.

You lie in wait, sleep
in dugouts. Everything
about your method of
approach relies on stealth.
Still, I'm grateful you've
postponed the bugle and
the charge.

This body is disputed land,
our mutual home. Surely
you dread each battle
as much as I.

You're a diplomat, I'll grant
you. Maybe I am too. But lines
have been drawn. In flesh
and blood, skin and bone.
We can't go back, old friend.
May I call you that? Would
you mind?

François

A stranger
has written to tell me how he felt,
what he thought
about my photos of urban trees,
holy sentries
                up against fences,
walls.

His letter flutters in my
untethered hand
as Nurse Joon scurries
toward my reclining leather chair
to check the tube, the drip, the cherry-colored,
Hades-laden
                flow.

One deep, slow breath. Today
I will not care
about needles that scar my veins, scare me
half to death.

François, a stranger,
loves my trees,
                and has written, from afar,
        to tell me so.

Lullaby to Tired

Rest your eyes, rest your eyes, like two
tired feet on the ottoman of Monday.
Rest your feet, rest your feet,
like two tired thighs on the settee
of Tuesday. Run a bath, step in water,
rest your knees in the tub of Thursday,
much as you would your head on
Friday's shoulder. (Oh where did
Wednesday go?) Rest your arms,
rest your arms as a hummingbird might
rest its wings after sipping from the
thousandth flower. Come Saturday,
come Sunday, rest your grief, rest your
grief, just as you'd rest your sweaty palm
on the staircase rail as it waits for you
to catch your breath, helps you up
to the top of tomorrow.

Thunderstorm at the Dinner Party

Her Highness, Mistress Thunder, crashed the dinner party,
swooped in wearing her best storm dress—a hybrid
of chatoyant silk, multiple orgasms, and a suit of armor.
Hello my dears! she roared. Lightning struck the clouds
and lit the sky with rebel neon. An invisible doorman banged
a gong. They murmured, ooh'd and ahh'd. *You'd think we were kids,*
said the guest who'd just had a tad of cancer snipped from his
hairy earlobe. *What's the big deal?* But dishes quaked, and ghosts
of kisses past flew out of the woodwork—firsts, lasts,
one-of-a-kinds, never-to-be-repeated's. Irksome nostalgia! Uninvited.
Their raconteur, who'd been telling a story about a girl named Margaret,
paused as car alarms went philharmonic. They sat perched
on the edges of their chairs, waiting for more bolts to skewer
memories, years. Margaret—a lace and leather chick
who walked her greyhound 'round the block while smoking a fat cigar —
had made them grin, reveal their yellowed teeth, yearn for more. More
whiskey, gin and french-fried potatoes. More pages, blank.
More Margarets in battle boots and corsets. More seamless skin
with not much written on it yet.

Monthly Transfusion

If only I'd been able to afford
that red dress in the window.
If only I'd saved up enough
for a brand new Mini Cooper
or European summer vacation.

It never occurred to me
when yearning for the goods
that someday I'd be pining
with so much more ferocity
for blood.

I Was Wrong

Sunlight bakes my thinning hair.
Through the open window
wafts a wig of balmy air.
Sixty years gone by, plus two.

You'd think I'd never felt the sun,
you'd think no other kiss or whisper
ever skimmed this skin.
A mockingbird takes on the dawn.

Repeat, repeat, he sings his stolen songs.
Repeat, repeat, from early morning on.
Tireless and alone at five a.m.,
he sings to us, the world, the universe.

He does this from atop a barren pole.
Burst of sun, trill and chirp, another
day gone by. Things I thought
would never be enough, are.

IV.

Do No Harm

Five blown out
the nurses said with shrugs.

As if they'd never pushed a needle
into a vessel before.

Poor harrowed veins.
Crimson blotches on her arm,

bruises black and blue.
So many forms of terrorism
unintended, well-meaning.

At home she crept to bed,
turned the TV on, hid.
And there a smiling monk appeared.

He gave a nod, sipped tea,
said the trick was to listen,
to listen deeply,

especially to the enemy.

She nodded, smiled,
listened hard. Martini glass idling
at her side, tiny olive sword
at rest against the rim.

Just Be Careful

A bell is ringing. If you answer,
a voice will travel through the air, respond.
Certain things must not be mentioned
(your income, your lesions). Yes,
you've entered a danger zone.
Yes, you are corporeal. Be careful.
Be wild. There's a singing in you,
but love . . . talk about a royal mess.
Be prepared to spelunk through
pitch black offices of hungers, desires.
Be ready to slink away, lick
bawling wounds. Maharishi says
make friends with strangers, forget
about maps and plans. You're holding
a crazy situation in the palm of your hand.
When it's gone, another will rush in.
See that gargoyle in the mirror? It's you!
Time for a pill, a nap. Every minute
could be a wolf in sheep's clothing or
vice versa. Hold on. Some knots
untie themselves. Broken
washing machines will spin again.
You enter an empty room and are told to
wait, someone will be with you soon.

In the Glow of Our Muted TV

We discard what's gone
or gone awry,
give thanks for beans, potatoes,
chicken crisply fried.

You mention a hinge that broke
at work, how painter Dave,
from his ladder perch,
almost fell through a picture window.

I muster my own breaking news:
papers shuffled, server glitch,
stomach troubles.

As we talk, a friend of ours with ALS
puts the final touch on his plan for
tomorrow: Pull the plug, ventilator off.
We don't know of this yet, but if we did,
I believe we'd stay the course.

I'd tell you how I added
a sprinkle of Mrs. Dash
to the chicken,
how I baked red potatoes,
drizzled in oil,
in a boat of aluminum foil.
You'd note how tight painter Dave
held on despite the pull
of his Pilsner gut. He
wasn't hurt, the day was saved,
remained intact.

The Day After Paris

First we hear the crash. Someone's
parked Lexus got smashed. No one
saw it happen (red Jeep Cherokee glimpsed
careening out of sight).

Neighbors band together over the wreck,
pretending to assess what can't be assessed,
mostly just relieved it doesn't belong
to one of us. Here come the police.

Back inside, Rainbow (from three houses down)
in her vintage hippy poncho, knocks, white-faced,
stuttering, something about who the driver was:
almost surely her long-time mechanic,
newly deemed bipolar.

He stole the license plates off her husband's
old Mercedes (well, probably), right before he
rammed the Lexus on purpose. *He might
come back, might have a gun, could maybe even
hurt someone. What should we do?*

Questions, not answers, crawl into my mouth
like night spiders. Oh Rainbow, little
long-haired, tie-dyed, throwback Rainbow,
who knows? We are still so tired from
lugging yesterday around.

Ringing

From the bread-basket we'd passed for years
around your table, your wife asked us each

please take, for a memento, a small brass
goat bell, and to *please ring* them

as she led us to the bare-branched copse
where, from a pillowcase, she would pour

your ashes into the hole your son had
hatchet-split the frozen ground to dig.

Keep ringing, as our twenty boot heels
beat a mud path through fields of snow-melt,

and old corn stubble. *Ring, please ring,*
past snarled barbed wire, cedar shake

barn shingles, wild grapevine
snaking through a rusted tractor seat.

Keep ringing, ringing, as the river
ran beside us, *ring please ring,*

though your grandson, four,
pressed his hands to his ears,

screaming for the ringing to stop.

Terminal Agitation

is the phrase they use
when a dying person
starts doing
crazy things
like cutting holes
in the hose that runs
from oxygen tank
to nose mask,

which is what
Randy's wife did
with a pair of scissors
in the middle
of the night.

Randy, who'd been
working late
in the den, heard
her babbling, and
ran down the hall
as fast as he could
to the bedroom
that had once been
their haven.

When she kept on
insisting that
she couldn't breathe
and needed him
to let her have
more air,
he pried the pair
of scissors
from her hand.

Wildfire

Drought and winds could give
a shit. Those who fight the flames
are spread thin as worn out veins
and tired down to the marrow.
Evacuation is the only option.
Leave everything behind. Seconds
are too tiny, decades too heavy.
Don't wait for the dog. You're
breathing in the ashes of other
people's houses, the hair of spooked
horses too freaked to get in vans.
It has eaten your left breast already,
flattened a town in your thigh. Now
it's headed for the woods—hips, ribs,
spine, blood. Did you hear me?
Are you deaf? I said forget the dog.

V.

Stage Four, 2010

Tomato sauce bubbling,
radio on, I'm spinning, gliding
over kitchen linoleum. Arias trill
from the scent of Italian parsley.
Strange, this singing while
picking dirty socks up off the floor,
this not bothering when
one goes missing, this new
knowing that lost socks
come back, Alakazam,
on their own.

Ode to My Newfound Euphoria

We grill. My gimpy leg gets dragged across our
drought-brown yard, cane ignored, toward a can

of lukewarm pop. The smell of fresh mown grass
is woven into a baby's blanket of air. Dungy old dog,

my protector. Husband in (notorious) floppy straw
hat, king of marinade, my hero. Beloved son, soon

to take his leave again, making guacamole. His
darling French girlfriend speaks lilting garble I can't

understand. I'm thrilled. Aluminum chairs, wobbling,
forever verging on tipping over, hold us. Freeway

decibels batter at the ailing fence—my castle wall,
invincible. Everyone coughs when they sidle too near

the fire. Danger. As it should be. Soon we're overrun
by shadows, fog. So what. A chill wind gusts in, we put

our arms around it. Corncobs in foil cradles get carried
to the dining room. Every knife, fork and spoon feels

just like a plan, good as cash under a mattress, crossed
fingers, an umbrella, precious pills stashed like jewels.

All of China

She had the face of a prison warden
and a thick waist, like a tire.
I wish I'd thanked her,
that woman who drove the taxi,
for what she let me read in her eyes.
I saw you clutch him in the doorway,
heard the wail behind your smile.
I'm a mother too. It'll be okay.

Then she whisked my child,
a young man now, off to China.

I would have thrown my arms around
her hefty shoulders for a few quick seconds.
We would have never said, or felt the need to say,
a word.

Yesterday, his hand was tucked in mine
as we strolled six blocks to his first day
of kindergarten, remembering to look
both ways at every corner.

How do I not fear all of China
now that he is there? Mayhem can happen
at any gong-filled festival,
cherry blossoms falling all over Tiananmen Square.

Won't he be too beautiful, too tall?
He'll draw undue attention, an isolated redwood
in a bonsai-crowded plaza full of fiery, trampled ghosts.

Water bottle he left on the table
clasped to my chest,
his hand slipping away yet again,
I am locked inside my heart for a while.

Mail Order Shoes

Soon the postman will come, my shoes in a box,
his feet on the steps, six thumps up, six more down.
I don't need them, of course.

Last week the neighbor's house caught fire,
this week the owner stands in a dumpster, sorting
through ashes and soot. Urban sirens howl their
rescue missions, moving closer, then farther away.
Be still, my jackhammer heart. Things burn. Let them.

I watch our local mockingbird through binoculars,
how his belly feathers soothe the splintered
wooden pole he sings from, how they flutter when
he leaps to screwball bouts of flight, three feet up,
wings akimbo, then back down.

In the transfusion room I take pictures of reflections
on linoleum as blood flows down to my arms.
How deeply red it is, as it drip drip drips then streams
through tubes in loops. As if I were being served
a fine claret from Bordeaux for five hours straight.

Street Cleaning Day

Jack looks like a normal guy. No one else is out
on the street, just him. He moves my car from Friday
to Monday, saving me from another ticket.

This is something he often does, two or three times
a week. I can see him in the fog, partly lit by street
lamps before blue morning glories open.

I watch him head out to work in his whites—that's
what they call a house painter's overalls. I can see
him, a beautiful phantom, with my eyes closed.

Impossibly

Pajama'd
at noon.
Hair askew.
Moving through
each hour
as though it were
recyclable.

Yet every day,
impossibly,
the beautifuls arrive.
The house painter's
scaffold net
billows in the wind.

The dog bites
our hand.
The dog licks
our hand.

Falling

No cure in sight, but I'm off my back and headed
out to walk around the block, reconnect with
jasmine blooms, exhaust fumes, burgers sizzling
on the neighbor's grill. My starry-eyed feet, bravely
naive, believe they've sprouted wings. As for me,
I never tire of watching leaves change colors as they die.
Exquisite little fans, they swirl to my toes like mystics
or cavorting drunks, as if falling were no big deal.
Often I stop, kneel and stare at their kaleidoscopic
graves, grateful to see no coffins. I take what I can get,
grab this chance to smile and say long time no see
to magnolias, maples, baby ginkgos that yesterday
risked bursting into kamikaze yellow after the belated
winter rain, after having been bare and gray so long
they couldn't stand another freezing, naked second.

VI.

Portuguese Macaroni

This is the first official visit since their deaths.
They've escaped from their urns, invited me over,
perhaps in honor of my 60th, and we are ensconced
at the Motel Six, just outside of nowhere.

I stand in their darkened room, curtains drawn,
with nothing much to see except the two of them
on a sagging double bed. They display a surprising
effervescence. "But why," I inquire, "are you here?"

"We already told you," says my dad, "Portuguese
macaroni. There's no other pasta like it. Nothing else
compares." "It's the best macaroni in the world,"
says Mom. "We've got a whole new business!"

"Go look! It's on ice!" The bathtub is filled to the brim.
What can I say? That I never knew they had it in them,
or that Portugal was the epicenter of specialty macaroni
manufacturing? That I fear I may be hallucinating?

Could this have to do with my caloric intake?
Or is it just some crazy pyramid scheme? But wait.
Perhaps they regret their pre-death coldness? Is ice
a metaphor, or just refrigeration? The landline rings.

My father races to answer. There are no chairs here,
so I remain upright. Let me insert that I have imagined
going to Portugal ever since I saw *Enchanted April*.
It was set in 1920s Italy, but at the time I thought it

was Portugal. It took place in a hotel castle on the shores
of the Mediterranean. Four European women on vacation,
all in flux—two wives, a widow and a vixen. A great deal
of drama ensued. Could I have missed some pivotal point,

some well-oiled macaroni hinge upon which the whole
plot turned? My father hangs up the phone and rejoins
my mother on the bed: "It's a specialty macaroni," he says.
They were never this happy. "It's *foreign*. It's *gourmet*."

Until Dusk

This morning I pretended
to be sleeping
when you went to the kitchen.
            I listened
as you made coffee, toasted
your English muffin.

I knew you were also making
a cup for me, my portion of
            the daily grind
carefully measured
and spooned into the filter.

After you'd gone, I shuffled
over cold linoleum,
poured the heated water,
            filled my cup, glad
to call the house my own
until dusk.

Years ago,
        two autumnal people
tired of being alone, we
took no vows,
        pooled our stuff,
got a pup,
            let the chips fall.

Waiting at the window now,
funny how long it takes
for dusk to come.

Ah there you are.
        Our old dog
pounds her tail.

Umbilical, 1983

I labored on the old yellow couch—
a shade of mustard I'll never
forget—and pushed until my face
flushed red with the blood we shared.

On the wall above my head, a painting
by Modigliani—a woman who resembled me
except for her eyes, which were closed
as if she slept, set apart from all
the bliss, the mess.

It was October—the sunniest
room of the house, where
back door opened onto apples,
and belly muscles turned inside out—
when your head finally crowned,
and you, my son, were stupendously born,
umbilical cord cut, yet not—
leaves churning, spinning beyond
the window, light playing at the edges
of spider lace curtains until it too
broke through to rapture.

Creeping to a Halt

Afterward we change the ravished sheets.
Billows go up then down in long slow flaps.
I get myself home, as usual, without any help
from him. I know how to build a perfect lonesome
bridge, exactly wide enough for one. In my kitchen
I scream at the grocery bag that has spilled itself
all over the place, made a royal mess. Oranges
on the table roll their eyes and sigh. My jaded
walls try not to say *we told you so*. My cat appears
from out of nowhere, stalking prey that only she
can see. She creeps to a halt between dustpan and
broom, stares at what she has her cat heart set on.
Belly flat to linoleum, she can't get any lower.

Bucket List

Absurdly assuming its diameter to be
that of a thermometer or skinny chopstick,
I stand with my back to the needle
while the doctor readies the syringe,
and summon a view of my inner Montana—
asylums of plain and sky, wild horse
terrain, then on to Utah canyons, desert
nights, coral sand dunes. The moment
it pierces my hip, enters muscle,
then veers off course and hits a nerve
(chances slim to none, they said) I know
something sacred is at stake. But what?
Life? I'm sick to death of being drained
and sad. Afterward, limping down one
infinite block, steadied by my husband's hand,
I pass shadows, sun, people, seagulls,
traffic, grass—more items on my bucket list.
Almost home, we embrace our urge, now
predictable, to stop and splurge on deli fare—
egg salad for me, chop suey for him.
Two bags of chips.

A Meeting

Tumor markers
on the rise again,
and so
I've made the leap
to somewhere
near a pack
of wolves
in Scandinavia.
Though
almost extinct,
their numbers
are up
from only a handful
to over
a hundred now.
I'm inching
toward the juncture
where one will
cross the snow
to greet me, as is
their nature.
I'll part my lips
as I've been taught,
and feel a tongue
on mine.

VII.

Undertow, Etcetera

My apprehension and I fear the undertow,
so avoid beaches, waves, blue ocean.

My tension and I struggle,
copacetic as a fistful of clocks.

Me and my contradictions feel wistful,
long for better grammar, the nondigital.

Neither I nor my depression are in the mood
for anemia. It keeps us from rearranging

the furniture. All of us require floods
of bright red hemoglobin to transport

our oxygen, and hordes of diehard platelets
to keep us stroke-free, lucid, clotting.

Dishwater laps against the sink.
Cups and plates—dozing, warm, calm—

soak peacefully. We all want to be just like them,
gently washed and dried. Carefully put away.

When I Was a Poem

After he turned me into a poem
He slipped me into a folder. How long did I lie
On that piece of paper? A second, an hour?
The time it took to boil an egg? The life span
Of an ant, a whale, a star? I can't remember. But after
Awhile—an inch, a mile, forever—it didn't matter.

When I was gone he pulled out the poem
He'd found in his trembling amygdala, a corner
That held his fear of never knowing my palm
On his cheek again, or hearing me say I loved
His skin whether prickly with stubble or smooth
As a bite of his perfectly cooked pink trout.

He read me out loud at the funeral. Some people
Laughed, others cried, a few remained dry-eyed,
Having already wandered off in their heads
Toward dinner. I stayed until his last word,
Drinking in the blink we'd been.

Then

       After, I'll be
a shadow or a
ray of sun,
a hurricane or wind,
lioness
              or rain,
flower or horse or
bee.

Or better yet,
          a tree—
      fruit bearer, leaf wearer,
rooted.

       Home for
mockingbird, starling, warbler.

           Whisperer
of rustle and breeze.

Shade-giver,
shadow-maker, sun-rippler.

Mother of
      oak, birch, ash,
cherry, pine.

           Then.

Bread Fight

It wouldn't go back into the bag. Not the way I wanted.
I had to shake it, hard. Had to shake it back into the bag
and yell, *Fuck you, you stupid piece of shit!* I put lots
of butter on the slab that I kept out to eat. I think that
helped my head. I'm not proud I lost my temper,
but I'm not ashamed either. There's nothing wrong
with a good fight, a good honest fight with a loaf
of cinnamon challah. Sticky with syrupy goop,
it clung to the sides of the bag, wouldn't slide.
I just couldn't stand there and take it, in front
of the broken dishwasher, like a sorry punching bag,
pummelled and made mute by some stuck-up, fresh-
baked (oh, excuse me, *hand-crafted*) loaf of fucking
asshole bread. Like I don't have enough on my plate.
Like I've got time to stand around being a wimp
of an excuse for a woman. I mean, I don't have
anything against this loaf, *per se*. It was the bread
and the bag *in conjunction*. Give 'em an inch and
you know what happens—you'll never get another
loaf back into another bag. Look at Ms. Steinem.
Have some respect. Am I not an Amazon, too?

Lists

When I still had more years
                    ahead than behind, I made
lists of all my lovers past. Anselm, Bill, Bob . . .
Sam, Ted, Tom . . .
            Once in a blue moon,
memory balks, and I cheat.
        When no names starting with N come to mind,
I add Naseem, though all
we ever shared were poems,
            one forgettable kiss, and the smell of beer
gone sour on his breath as we
         bounced in the bed
of a rickety pickup truck on our way to . . .
I forget.
              Now I make lists
of the dead, of everyone I've
known or at least been
            interested in.
       I leap around, from my baby brother
who didn't reach forty, to that actress
           whose name I can never remember,
      the one with a slightly
crooked smile. Last time I googled her
              I found she'd
been dead three years,
from leukemia she'd had for more than twenty.

      Today I'm set on recalling my
dead neighbor's name.
      Long white beard, obese,
a hoarder, used a cane then a walker. His back yard
      faced onto ours,

was an overgrown mess. His pale pink roses,
long untended,

                petals brown around the edges,
cascaded over the fence we shared.

Oh, I remember now. Pat. His name was Pat. He lived
             in that house forty years,
     always wore a wide-brimmed straw hat,
would pass by our yard coming back from his walk,
      stop to pet our dog,
                catch his breath.

Destiny

When Wasn't-Meant-to-Be
had the epiphany
that she could be Meant-to-Be,
could drop the Wasn't
and be who she was
and was meant to be,
was that ever a surprise.

When she (determiner
of was's and wasn'ts) became
(that is,
allowed herself to become)
the one-breasted woman
that she was
(and was meant to be)
rather than continue
to try and be
the two-breasted woman
that she once had been
(and had been meant to be)
well gee, was that also
ever a surprise.

Porch Light

Winter light fading, husband and dog gone
for a walk, they'll be back in an hour.
If the sky goes dark, I turn the porch light on.

Exhausted after working all day long,
he's devoted to home, hearth, his other.
Winter light fading, husband and dog gone

up the hill, where our terrier girl loves to run.
Her ecstasy filled me when I was able to take her.
If the sky goes dark, I turn the porch light on.

Simple daily things, those are our song
of love despite the trials of growing older.
Winter light fading, husband and dog gone

off together, leaving me here alone,
wishing I too could have skipped out the door.
If the sky goes dark, I turn the porch light on.

They fill in what I lack, trek along
the streets, stop for snacks at the corner store.
Winter light fading, husband and dog gone.
When my heart goes dark, I turn the porch light on.

ABOUT THE AUTHOR

As the founder of *The Writing Salon*, a unique creative writing school in San Francisco and Berkeley that she directed for 16 years, Jane Underwood was a beloved mentor. Her poetry, essays and erotica appeared in *The San Francisco Chronicle, Salon, The Sun Magazine*, and *Best Women's Erotica*, and she was also a gifted photographer. After being diagnosed with cancer in 2005, she kept an online blog at "My Great Breast Cancer Adventure," and returned to her early love of poetry with renewed purpose. The manuscript of this book was on her nightstand when she died in February, 2016.

www.ingramcontent.com/pod-product-compliance
Lightning Source LLC
Chambersburg PA
CBHW032028090426
42741CB00006B/776